The Big Book
of
Brain Games

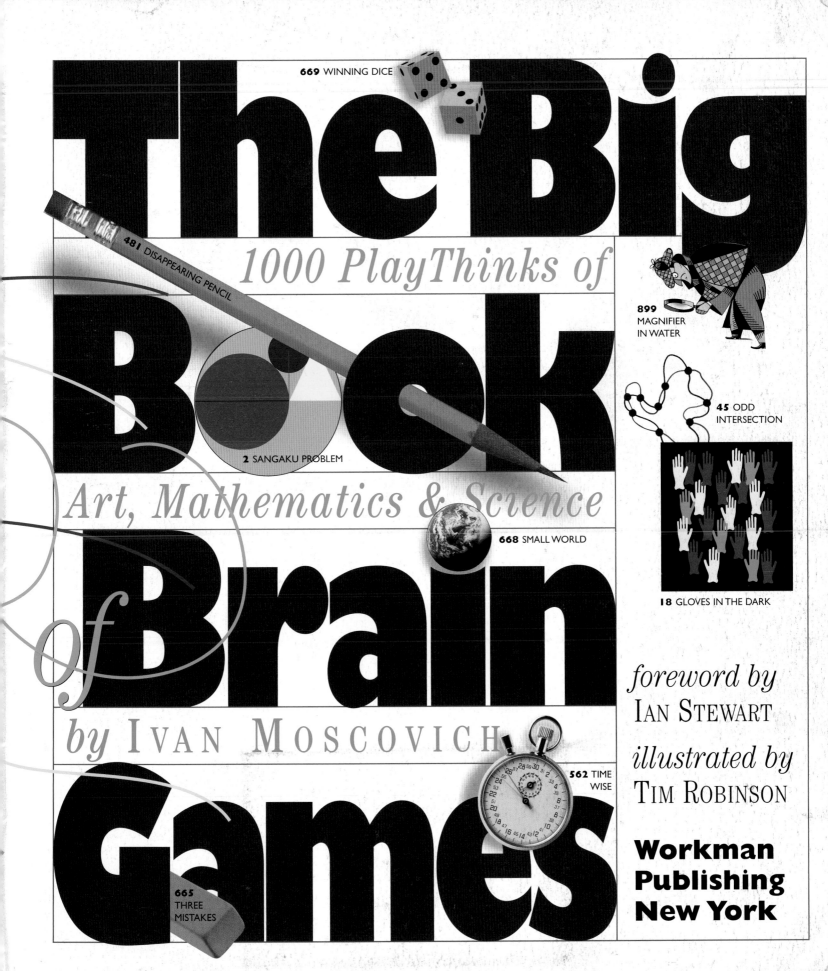

The Big Book of Brain Games

1000 PlayThinks of

Art, Mathematics & Science

by I VAN M O S C O V I C H

669 WINNING DICE

481 DISAPPEARING PENCIL

899 MAGNIFIER IN WATER

2 SANGAKU PROBLEM

45 ODD INTERSECTION

668 SMALL WORLD

18 GLOVES IN THE DARK

562 TIME WISE

665 THREE MISTAKES

foreword by I AN S TEWART

illustrated by T IM R OBINSON

Workman Publishing New York

This book is a labor of love.
I dedicate it to my wife, Anitta,
with love and gratitude for
her infinite patience, valuable
judgment and assistance;
to my daughter, Hila, who is
my harshest but fairest critic
and continually inspires me
with new insights and ideas;
and to all those who like games,
puzzles, surprises and challenges.

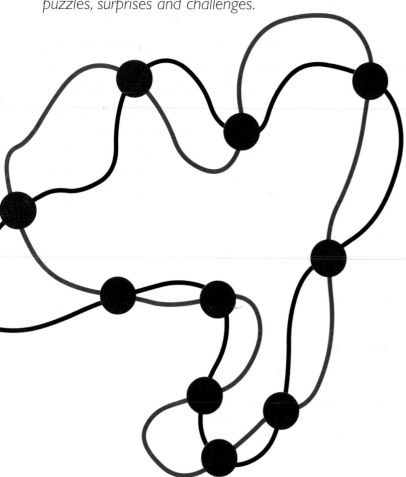

Library of Congress Cataloging-in-Publication Data is available.
ISBN-13: 978-0-7611-3466-4
ISBN-10: 0-7611-3466-2

Workman books are available at special discounts when purchased in bulk for premiums and sales promotions as well as for fund-raising or educational use. Special editions can also be created to specification. For details, contact the Special Sales Director at the address below.

Typesetting by Barbara Peragine

Workman Publishing Company, Inc.
708 Broadway
New York, NY 10003-9555
www.workman.com

First Printing April 2006

10 9 8 7 6 5 4 3 2 1

PlayThink 88, "Lost in Caves," from "The Road Coloring Problem," by Daniel Ullman. Reprinted by permission from The Mathematical Association of America, *The Lighter Side of Mathematics,* edited by Richard K. Guy and Robert E. Woodrow, page 105.

PlayThink 342, "Sharing Cakes"; PlayThink 161, "Multi-Distance Set"; PlayThink 339, "Japanese Temple Problem from 1844," from *Which Way Did the Bicycle Go?,* by Joseph D.E. Konhauser, Dan Velleman and Stan Wagon. Reprinted by permission from The Mathematical Association of America, *Which Way Did the Bicycle Go?,* pages 62, 68 and 107.

Thanks to Greg Frederickson, for permission to use several of his polygon transformation dissections, "Heptagon Magic," "Pentagonal Star," "Nonagon Magic" and "Twelve-Pointed Star" (PlayThinks 42, 479, 478 and 483); to Richard Hess, for the idea behind "Measuring Globe" (PlayThink 810); to Ian Stewart, for the illustration for "Goats and Peg-Boards" (PlayThink 309); and to the late Mel Stover, for his geometrical vanishing illusion, "Disappearing Pencil" (PlayThink 481).

Photo credits: PlayThink 585, "Jekyll and Hyde" (page 213), courtesy of Photofest; PlayThink 907 "Archimedes's Mirrors" (page 310), courtesy of the New York Public Library Picture Collection.

ACKNOWLEDGMENTS

First and foremost, I would like to thank Martin Gardner for Everything. His work, personality and friendship have been my inspiration since the mid-fifties, when I read his first "Mathematical Games" column in the first issue of *Scientific American*. His immense contribution to the popularization of recreational mathematics (and mathematics in general) has created an environment of creativity. Without him, there would have been many fewer International Puzzle Parties and mathematical exhibitions, and certainly no Gatherings for Gardner, an event like no other.

Over the last forty years or so, these conventions of like-minded souls have allowed me to meet "Martin's People," a diverse group of mathematicians, scientists, puzzle collectors, magicians and inventors unified by a fascination with mind games and a love of recreational mathematics. They have provided me with endless hours of enjoyment and intellectual enrichment and, very often, precious friendship. My appreciation and thanks to all of them, mentioning just a few: Paul Erdös, my famous relative, who provided the first sparks; David Singmaster, with whom I dreamed of a very special puzzle museum; Ian Stewart for his early help; John Horton Conway, Solomon Golomb, Frank Harary, Raymond Smullyan, Edward de Bono, Richard Gregory, Victor Serebriakoff, Nick Baxter; Greg Frederickson, for his beautiful dissections; Al Seckel, Jacques Haubrich, Lee Sallows, Jerry Slocum, Nob Yoshigahara, James Dalgety, Mel Stover, Mark Setteducati, Bob Neale, Tim Rowett, Scott Morris, Will Shortz, Bill Ritchie, Richard Hess and many, many others.

I owe a debt of gratitude to the work of pioneers—Sam Loyd, Henry Dudeney, many others—whose early books provided so much inspiration. In a way, *The Big Book of Brain Games* is a visual synthesis of the whole of recreational mathematics.

Finally, thanks to Peter Workman, for his enthusiastic, ego-boosting reaction to the first crude color dummy of *PlayThinks,* which I so timidly presented to him; to Sally Kovalchick, who got things started, and to Susan Bolotin, who finished them; to Nick Baxter and Jeffrey Winters for their help with math, science and language; and to others at Workman, all so professional, including (but certainly not limited to) Paul Hanson, Elizabeth Johnsboen, Malcolm Felder, Patrick Borelli, Janet Parker, Eric Ford, Mike Murphy, Barbara Peragine, Anne Cherry and Kelli Bagley.

I. M.

CONTENTS

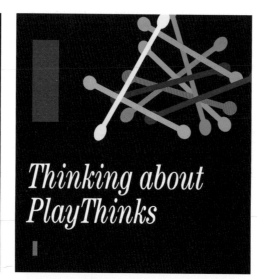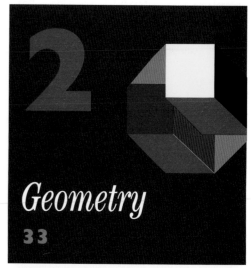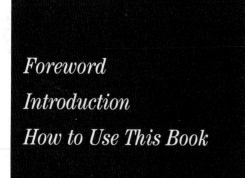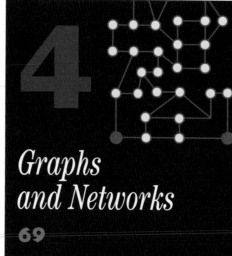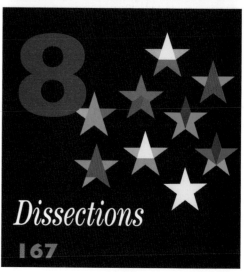

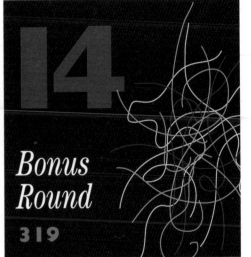

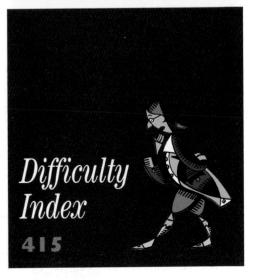

FOREWORD

I wrote the "Mathematical Recreations" column of *Scientific American* for ten years, and it was in that capacity, as a gamesman (and not as the mathematician I am), that I first encountered Ivan Moscovich. It was 1984, and I was helping to write the text for his book *Ivan Moscovich's Super-Games*. I was immediately struck by his trademarks: cheerful, attractive graphics, and puzzles that are genuinely fun to work on and—with luck and hard work—to solve.

Puzzles, like many things in the realm of the intellect, are deceptively simple. They belong, so it seems, to a fantasy world full of shapes made from matchsticks, weird tiles meant to be arranged in ridiculous ways and odd numerical curiosities. Real life, we say, is not like that. The problems we encounter in our daily lives are more subtle, less clearly defined, less artificial.

Nonsense.

I don't mean that real-life problems aren't subtle; I don't mean that when we run into them they come to us with a logical plan. And I don't mean they're artificial—at least, not any more artificial than the peculiar world humanity has built for itself and fondly imagines is the natural order of things. No, what I mean is this: even simple puzzles are more subtle, less clearly defined and less artificial than they appear.

Lurking within every good puzzle is a general message about how to think when you are confronted with a problem. Even if the puzzle itself is posed in a simplified world, the way that you have to think to solve it is often useful in more significant areas of human activity. It's great. You can enjoy yourself building fences to separate four cats who live on a square grid (even though no self-respecting cat would sit still while you fenced it in) and at the same time refine your understanding of "area." You can roll dice and brush up on statistics. Or you can amuse yourself with a few coins and discover the deep mathematics of "even and odd."

Speaking of mathematics: If ever there was an area of human activity where apparently simple puzzles could open up the hidden depths of the universe, mathematics is it. For instance, one of the current frontiers of mathematical research is knot theory. On the surface, this is about how you decide whether a knot in one piece of string can be rearranged until it forms what looks like a different knot in another piece of string. Who could possibly use such a theory? Who would need it? Boy Scouts? Fishermen?

The answer is that a lot of things can be knotted—not just string. Knots are just the simplest examples in a vast area of mathematics with applications throughout science. Molecules of DNA are often knotted, and if you can recognize which knots arise in which circumstances, you can learn a great deal about their underlying biology and chemistry. There are knotlike objects in quantum mechanics, too, so an effective theory of knots can tell us about the fundamental nature of the universe.

Knot theory isn't confined to string any more than magnetic theory is confined to helping people find their way. Its simplicity is not a *restriction* on its applicability; rather, in mathematics, the simpler a concept is, the more fundamental it is likely to be. Think of numbers. They're simple, but we use them everywhere. And that's as it should be, since the simpler a tool is, the more uses it is likely to have.

The art of the mathematician is to derive far-reaching consequences from apparently simple material. And the people who best appreciate this started playing with puzzles as children. Puzzles help your mathematical imagination to develop; I *know* they helped mine. They help you learn to think in generalities, not just simpleminded specifics. They help you understand that by thinking about tangled lengths of string, you can make far-reaching discoveries in biology and physics.

This is why Ivan's new book, like the rest of his lifework, is so important. Because it shows you that puzzles are intimately involved in every aspect of life, art, science, culture. And because it makes mathematical thinking painless, interesting and fun.

Ian Stewart
Coventry, England

INTRODUCTION

I am a lover of games. Over the last forty years I have collected, designed and invented thousands upon thousands of them—hands-on interactive exhibits, puzzles, toys, books, you name it. One of the reasons I'm so passionate about games is that I believe they can change the way people think. They can make us more inventive, more creative, more artistic. They can allow us to see the world in new ways. They can inspire us to tackle the unknowable. They can remind us to have fun.

That's why I wrote this book.

Like so many who lived through the twentieth century, I have witnessed repeated attempts to snuff out humanity's creative spark—and not just by political tyrants. I have seen the creative impulse wither away in schools. I have seen it devalued at work. And along the way I have learned that to become fully free, our society must do more than repel dictators. We must encourage what is best—and what is most human—within ourselves.

I believe that one of the most effective ways to foster that special part in each of us is through play. Child psychologists have long known that children learn about the world through games; now it is time to extend that model to adults. We can understand the most abstract and difficult concepts if we allow ourselves the luxury of approaching them not as work, but as fun—and a form of exploration.

People have always felt the pull to explore new worlds, and now that most of the physical frontiers have been crossed, the mental ones should beckon us. Too often, though, we act as if challenges to the mind are too difficult to contemplate. We judge the effort needed to push into new mental territories as simply too great. And so we turn back.

It is at the place where self-doubt and fear threaten to derail our urge to explore that play becomes a truly important activity. Seeing hard work as fun is what keeps the amateur athlete training for the marathon, and it is what keeps a child or an adult struggling to find the answer to a puzzle. At the end of the race, the runner dwells in a place of pride. At the end of the game, the puzzle solver feels smart, successful and at one with the beauty of mathematics.

Shortly after I emigrated to Israel in 1952, I began planning one of the first science museums in which the exhibits invited the visitor to participate. That interactive concept became the model for many later museums, including the world-famous Exploratorium in San Francisco. At these museums, children and adults alike feel their minds wake up: they suddenly grasp concepts previously rejected as "too difficult" or "impossible to understand." Doing the "problem" is fun, and so they understand it.

The activities in this book, which combine entertainment and brain teasing, expand on that idea and apply it to concepts common to art, science and mathematics. Because they transcend puzzles and games in the traditional sense, I have given them a new name: PlayThinks. A PlayThink may be a visual challenge, riddle or puzzle; it may be a toy, game or illusion; it may be an art object, a conversation piece or a three-dimensional structure. Some of the puzzles are completely original, while others are novel adaptations of classic and modern challenges. Whatever its form, a PlayThink will ideally transfer you to a state of mind where pure play and problem solving coexist.

Because playing and experimenting with PlayThinks stimulate creative thinking, you may find the book slyly educational. I certainly hope so! My goal is for you to play the games, solve the problems and come away more curious, more inventive, more intuitive. Enjoy!

Ivan Moscovich
Nijmegen, the Netherlands

HOW TO USE THIS BOOK

In my experience a single presentation of a mathematical idea generally fails to produce a lasting impression. On the other hand, interactive games and puzzles can make even the most advanced concepts understandable.

PlayThinks are designed to permit easy access to many ideas, in different contexts and at different levels. You will notice that many of them draw on the same set of ideas—probability, say, or graphing—with each one developing the concept more fully than the last. You may find that by attacking the PlayThinks in order, you can build up an understanding of a field of knowledge.

But that is far from the only way to use this book. Each PlayThink is rated in difficulty from 1 to 10. You might decide to do all the puzzles rated 1 and 2, they try the ones rated 3 and 4, and thus build up your abilities as a problem solver. (To find puzzles at your level, check the index at the back of the book.)

You might jump around in the book, first taking on the subjects that interest you most until you are ready to work your way deeper into the frontiers of what you think you don't know.

Or, using the key at the top of each puzzle as your guide, you might try all the mind puzzles (look for the ◉), then the pencil and paper puzzles (✎), and finally the more complicated ones that involve tracing or copying (▤) and cutting (✂). You can do the solo activities when you've got a few minutes by yourself, and pull out the group games and puzzles when you're with friends. You get the idea: it's all up to you. Just don't forget to play.